REGISTERED
TRADEMARK

select. **secure.** sustain.

REGISTERED TRADEMARK

The Business Owners' Essential
Guide to Brand Protection

CHERYL LORRAINE HODGSON

BRANDAIDE®|PRESS

Distributed by Brandaide Press
Brandaide is a registered trademark of Chipotle Entertainment, LLC.

Book Design: Charles McStravick

This publication is designed to provide accurate and authoritative information in regard to the subject matter covered. It is sold with the understanding that the publisher and author are not engaged in rendering legal, accounting, or other professional services. If legal advice or other expert assistance is required, the services of a competent professional should be sought.

Publisher's Cataloging-In-Publication Data

Hodgson, Cheryl.
Registered trademark : the business owners' essential guide to brand protection /
Cheryl Hodgson --1st ed.
ISBN: 978-0-9988826-2-8

Printed in the United States of America

❝ Being good in business is
the most fascinating kind of art.
Making money is art
and working is art
and good business
is the best art.

— ANDY WARHOL

CONTENTS

PREFACE

THE BUSINESS OWNERS' ESSENTIAL GUIDE TO BRAND PROTECTION empowers you to successfully protect and grow your business, including brand assets, by securing the benefits of protection from registered trademarks. Business owners, marketing, advertising and branding teams, together with general legal counsel, will learn how to use registered trademarks as a cost-effective way to immunize the life of a brand against today's many cyber threats. Registered trademarks serve to carve out market rights and increase the bottom line.

Most important, the Guide provides a simple three-step plan, which when followed, will greatly increase the chances of securing registered trademarks to immunize the life of your brand and serve as the foundation for sustaining your brand legacy.

Most every business now markets products and services online. We have truly moved from the world of bricks to clicks. As the Internet grew, most industries were turned on their ear. In today's digital marketplace, brand survival without strong online marketing is far from assured. As brands moved from "Bricks to Clicks," the traditional limited notions of brand protection flew out the window. The Internet ®evolution forced an evolution in brand protection upon both clients and the professionals who guide them. An entirely new set of reasons to secure and sustain strong brand protection arose, even more important than the existing ones.

I have practiced trademark, copyright, and entertainment law since graduating from law school. As a young attorney, I began my career as an associate on the biggest trademark jury verdict in history. Years later, my own legal skills and knowledge were challenged when the world got connected. Traditional legal principles simply didn't contemplate threats that could destroy an entire business with the click of a mouse.

Today's online brands must now vaccinate themsleves against cyber squatters, domain hijackings, typosquatting, trademarks as AdWords, and blatant theft of content. These are practices unheard of a few years ago. Many clients are still unaware of how these online threats destroy brand value and reputation and even threaten the very existence of their business.

I have had the privilege to represent authors, publishers, and consumer brands who were pioneers in navigating the global online marketplace. Some of the challenges they faced gave me the opportunity to recover domain names from hijackers, counsel clients in global registration strategies, and file or defend numerous federal court cases involving everything from wine brands to entertainers whose names were stolen. I have also developed licensing programs for brands whose services have expanded around the globe and registered countless trademarks, including solving problems for clients who received bad advice from unqualified "experts."

What came forward loudly and clearly is that much of the pain, loss, and expense clients experienced could have been avoided. Had these clients followed the right steps early in the life of their brand, including finding and following professional guidance, their outcomes would have been different. A small investment early in the life of the business to sustain the life of your brand, and create a lasting legacy is but a pittance compared to the cost of failing to do so.

There many well-qualified trademark professionals available to guide business owners. However, it is not always easy to find those professionals, or know whether the one they have hired is really competent to do the job. There is also the dark side. There are now a host of unregulated, unqualified firms offering filing services that mislead and even scam clients out of money, providing either bad advice or none at all.

I acknowledge the clients whose challenges provided me hard-earned experience and knowledge with which to write this Guide. I am most grateful to Reid Tracy and the Hay House team, who were pioneers in digital marketing for the books of dozens of the Hay House authors around the globe. Their innovation provided me the platform from which to recognize and solve the problems addressed in this guide.

I also wish to acknowledge Dana Arak and Michelle Parsons for their assistance. They are the next generation of experts, who I had the privilege of mentoring early in their careers. Mario Salinas, another Internet pioneer, unfairly lost his own business when he failed to register his brand name. Together we share Mario's experience in order to inform your own journey. Last but not least, my first mentor, Norma Core, gave me my first taste of the law at age 16. Her love and encouragement gave me the courage to pursue and realize my goals to achieve something greater than I ever dreamed possible.

To get the most from this Guide, go to **https://brandaide.com/vaxplan**. You will want to keep this planning guide handy to develop your own brand protection plan as you complete each chapter. There are three simple steps:

Select. Secure. Sustain.™

Once you have completed your protection plan, you will have a clear road map of what to protect, how to protect it, and a plan to grow and sustain its value for the long run. Let's get started!

CHAPTER

1

INTRODUCTION

BUSINESS OWNERS AND ENTREPRENEURS face complex business and legal challenges when building a profitable business. One of those challenges is to create and protect valuable intangible business assets, including registered trademarks.

For the first time, an experienced trademark attorney has developed a simple, easy to follow guide to develop and protect your brand assets. Registered trademarks are a valuable tool to vaccinate your brand with a three step plan. The goal is to create a strong, memorable brand that help makes an impact upon the lives of those you serve.

Select. Secure. Sustain.™

The tried and proven principles of trademark registration in this guide have been carefully reimagined to arm business owners and entrepreneurs with the tools necessary to develop and sustain a best-in-class brand. You will learn why registered trademarks are vital to your business and you will learn the keys to unlock the doors to approval of your applications. You will also learn pitfalls to avoid and how to find a trusted adviser who will mentor you with strength and integrity.

IN THIS INTEGRITY-DRIVEN GUIDE, YOU WILL LEARN:

- ➤ What is a trademark, and why and when you should seek to secure a registration.

- ➤ How to **select** a name that can be registered and enforced.

- ➤ The process to successfully **secure** a registered trademark.

- ➤ Reasons your application will be refused and ways you can avoid rejection.

- ➤ How to avoid being misled or scammed by dishonest opportunists.

- ➤ How to sidestep bad advice and find an expert you can trust.

- ➤ How to **sustain** the life of your brand following successful registration.

❝ Intangible assets are important to the value of any business.

Before diving in, let's set the stage of where and how trademarks fit in to your overall business plan. Almost everyone understands that hard assets like real estate, vehicles, and inventory are assets of the business. Intangible assets, while less widely understood, are often even more valuable when it comes to increasing the bottom line of your business.

Intellectual Property (IP) is especially important when it comes time to look for investors for your company or prepare for the sale of your business. In my experience, investors and purchasers are much more interested in knowing what Intellectual Property assets you've secured over the years than they are in knowing about depreciated assets and inventory. The first question a potential investor or prospective purchaser is likely to ask is *What's your IP protection?*

Registered trademarks are one of the most valuable assets of any successful business and are but one type of IP, albeit a vital one. Securing registered trademarks for brand names is a cost-effective form of insurance that reduces business risk with minimum legal expense. In addition, a portfolio of registered trademarks has proven to increase the value of the business.

My career as a brand protection attorney is filled with stories of smart clients who didn't seek or find proper guidance, or who simply didn't think it important. Some lost protection for their big ideas that were scooped up by third parties. Others got sued for using a name they failed to clear. They learned the hard way. As the idiom goes, "An ounce of prevention is worth a pound of cure."

❝ Obtain legal protection for brand names without being duped or misled.

Obtaining federal trademark protection doesn't need to be overly complicated or expensive. However, it's important to understand the basics and, in some cases, save precious resources by engaging expert counsel you can trust to do the job correctly the first time. In the first chapter, you will learn exactly what a trademark is, and whether your business needs one.

Supporting entrepreneurs in business is my passion. Empowerment to make wiser choices through knowledge and education is the foundation of my own experience. It is my sincere intention and desire to support a vital aspect of your business, inspiring you to protect your valuable ideas and intangible assets. Learn to insure those assets with a plan, including one to secure registered trademarks that will serve as a potent weapon when needed, and build a portfolio of valuable intangible assets that increase profits and create a sustainable brand legacy.

WHAT IS A TRADEMARK, AND WHY DOES YOUR BUSINESS NEED ONE?

A REGISTERED TRADEMARK CAN BE SECURED for a word, logo, slogan, symbol, color, or trade dress that is **distinctive** and serves to identifies your product or service to the public, and distinguish that product or service from others. Brands, and the registered trademarks that represent them, serve as messengers of a brand's core values. Great brands and the associated trademarks are carefully calculated to create an emotional connection to the consumer, and to establish consumer awareness and brand loyalty. Brands are valuable assets that must be nurtured and protected, like any other valuable asset.

The key word when seeking protection for a brand name is "distinctive." The word "distinctive" has special meaning when it comes to trademarks. As we will learn shortly, if the words or phrase you seek to register are not distinctive, they are not a trademark at all and are incapable of being registered or enforced.

The legal right to register and own trademarks is based upon the public policy of protecting consumers and the public from deception as to the source of the products or services they buy. Trademark protection provides the consumer with a means of distinguishing one company's product or service from another. In short, brand owners are permitted to register a trademark based upon the need to prevent consumer confusion in the marketplace.

For example, when it comes to your mobile phone, whether you choose a Samsung or an iPhone, the brand name, when protected as a registered trademark helps tell one phone from another.

Local businesses operating in a small geographic area, such as a dry cleaner, a floral shop, or a corner grocery don't typically need a registered trademark. Companies using descriptive or generic phrases for their product or service are also not likely candidates for a trademark, since descriptive or generic phrases don't qualify for protection as a trademark. We discuss the types of trademarks and what can be protected in greater detail in Chapter Two.

Companies selling products or services online and off across a larger geographical area may well benefit from a registered trademark.

Here are some points to consider when evaluating your own business needs.

WHY SHOULD YOU REGISTER?

Goods and services are marketed across more platforms than ever before. Traditional media such as radio, television, and print advertising are still important marketing and advertising outlets. However, nearly every business also markets services or sells products through websites and uses social media to increase their reach. With these ever-increasing platforms come new threats and more reasons to make certain the names of products and services are properly registered.

Does your company also market its services online or sell products over the Internet to customers in a variety of geographic locations? If so, then your business will benefit from the protection of a federal trademark registration. A registered trademark is like a vaccination for your brand. It's an inexpensive, preventive measure that helps get rid of a host of brand afflictions that plague online brands.

Perhaps the best way to understand the benefits of a registered trademark is by seeing what can happen when you fail to stake out a claim by timely filing to register a trademark for the goods or services your business provides to the consumer.

BOOKS, BULLIES & BIG RIVERS:
A real-life trademark drama

What do an online bookseller, a trademark bully, and the world's largest river have in common? They are the characters in Mario's brand story, one that had no happy ending. Mario lost his business because he failed to register a trademark when he launched his company in 1999. Mario made the all too common mistake of thinking he was adequately protected because he had registered a domain name.

Mario agreed that I should share his story so business owners just like you might learn from what happened to him. The story demonstrates the importance of staking out your exclusive right to sell certain goods and services by means of a trademark registration, and what can happen when you don't.

I first met Mario years earlier when he asked that I help negotiate a musical artist recording company agreement for a singer-songwriter he had produced. For many years, Mario had owned one of the top recording studios in the Los Angeles area, Milagro Sound. A recording engineer by training, Mario had overseen recordings by major Latin artists including *Los Calientes*, Juan Gabriel, *Los Bukis* and Gloria Trevi, and Joan Sebastian.

Some years later, Mario decided it was time for new horizons. He sold Milagro Sound, ready to join the Internet ®evolution that was taking the world by storm. The Internet had arrived, and everyone was trying to get connected.

By the end of 1996, there were a mere 36 million users online—not large by today's standards. Then, in 1999, Apple released its AirPort wireless router and built Wi-Fi connectivity into their new Macs. This and other products helped begin the popularization of cable-free connections at work and home. We were all becoming connected—moving beyond the slow dial-up connections: "You've got mail."

It was the dawn of a new era. Computers were changing the lives of everyone. We were all trying to understand and join the Internet. Mario created a business to focus on the Internet and use his talents to help others connect to the World Wide Web. Mario jumped online too, launching a new company to provide web design and computer networking services for consumers and businesses.

In May 1999, Mario registered a domain that incorporated the name of a well-known river. The landing page of his website prominently featured a photo of the river. Mario selected the name since it seemed like a great metaphor for the jungle that was the Internet. Mario wasn't thinking in terms of building or protecting a brand. He didn't understand the importance or value of registering a trademark to stake out his territory. Early Internet marketers were more concerned about scooping up generic or descriptive domains as a substitute for trademark protection. That was and still is a misguided notion when it comes to building an online brand.

But Mario was not the only one who thought the river was a great name. In 1998, at about the same time Mario launched his business, another startup began selling books on the Internet. The little online bookseller happened upon the same river as a metaphor for the power of the Internet and launched an online store selling books.

By 2005, there were one *billion* people online. Mario's business had grown, but his was a personal services business. His size was no match for the online bookseller that had grown rapidly and was now selling a lot more than books. The little online bookstore had become a giant—Amazon.com.

That same year, Mario began receiving threatening letters from a large Los Angeles law firm, demanding that he turn over his domain names (amazonnetworks.com and amazon-networks.com) and change the name of the business he had operated for six years. There was no offer of a buyout. This was a hardcore shakedown with threats and intimidation. I know. I defended him.

When Mario's answer was not an immediate yes, Amazon sued Mario. Mario didn't just get sued a little. Amazon sued big time. In May 2005, Amazon filed a lawsuit in the U.S. Federal Court in Los Angeles, falsely accusing Mario of trademark infringement and unfair competition. Mario was unfairly labeled with the new bad-guy term: "cyber squatter." Nothing could have been further from the truth, but at the time, even the meaning of "cyber squatter" was still unknown in legal circles.

Back in 1999 when Mario launched, he had every right to register a trademark for the mark "Amazon" for the services that he provided. But Mario made a costly mistake, an error in judgment that would cost him his business. Mario failed to do what the big dogs do: mark his territory and stake out his claim. Mario could have easily registered the word "Amazon" for web design and computer networking services. There was no risk of confusion with Amazon who was selling only books and Mario who was installing computer network systems. Had he obtained a registered trademark for AMAZON NETWORKS, his story would have had a happier ending. After all, at the time they both launched, Amazon was selling books, and the Amazon River was better known than a startup online bookseller. Amazon was not yet any more famous than Mario was, and it had created no legal rights in the name for the services Mario provided to the public. Even by the time Amazon sued Mario in 2005, it had no valid legal rights to use the term in his field.

Mario was innocent, and he had legal rights. He had chosen the name Amazon in good faith, and his services were unrelated to those of Amazon.com. Still, in its complaint against Mario, Amazon rewrote history to suit its own agenda, ignoring Mario's valid rights to the name (See page 95 for a copy of the actual lawsuit served on Mario). Mario had no registered trademark to prove his exclusive rights to the name for the services he provided.

Without the registration, the cost of proving his rights was enormous. Like most young companies, Mario didn't have $100,000 or more to defend his rights against a well-funded public company. A modest investment when he launched would have saved his business six years later, or led to a fair buy out of his rights.

In the end, Mario gave up the Amazon domain names for a pittance, a fraction of what he should have received had he obtained a registered trademark to protect his business.

Two valuable lessons emerge from the ashes of Amazon Networks. First, common law rights are not adequate protection for companies marketing branded products and service in the digital marketplace. This means relying on a domain name is not enough.

Second, a registered trademark doesn't just give the owner the right to stop third parties from poaching. The registration stakes out the owner's own territory or "zone of protection" for the goods and services being sold, and for the class of customers to whom they are marketed and sold.

As of this writing, there are an estimated 4.39 billion people connected to the Internet, and that number is growing daily. In today's Internet jungle, protection for your brand is not a luxury, it's a fundamental necessity for the life of your business. With these in mind, let's examine the benefits of a registered trademark in greater detail.

Registration Stakes Out Your Claim for Use of a Brand Name for Specific Goods and Services

Once a trademark registration issues, the owner is entitled to nationwide legal rights to use the trademark for the goods and services claimed in the registration and that are being sold to the public. By staking out your claim for the goods and services you sell, you will prevent a third party from using the same or similar name for the identical or even related goods and services. Without a registration for your goods and services, the opposite is likely to occur. A third party can obtain the registration and threaten your business even if you used the name first. This was Mario's dilemma as to computer services.

Registration Provides Constructive Notice

Trademark registration is like recording title to the house you purchase, allowing you to kick trespassers out quickly and with minimal expense. A trademark registration provides constructive notice to the world of the trademark owner's rights. Ignorance is no defense for a third party who adopts the same or a confusingly similar name to one that is federally registered.

Constructive notice is a concept most people understand when the deed to their house is recorded; the same applies to trademarks. Constructive notice is a legal substitute for *actual* notice. Actual notice means, "I personally told you." When it comes to property, both real and personal, you cannot personally tell everyone in the world of your claim to ownership. As a result, the law allows the owner to record a claim of ownership in a public agency where third parties are responsible for searching the public records. That's exactly what the Trademark Office records do. They serve as constructive notice of the owner's rights in the mark. As we discuss in Chapter Six, a market and legal search prior to filing is a vital step in prefiling planning.

Domain Names Can Infringe Your Trademark Rights

The most common form of business theft of trademarks in today's global market occurs online. One type of theft involves infringing domains containing someone else's brand name in the URL. Trademark infringement in a domain occurs when a third party uses your trademark to offer competing goods or services. Infringement occurs not only when someone is selling directly competitive products or hijacks your URL. Infringement also occurs in the case of Pay Per Click Ads (PPCs), typo squatting (deliberate mis-spellings of trademarks to divert traffic), and purchase of trademarks as Google AdWords by competitors. These are but three examples.

There are streamlined legal procedures to stop registra-tion of domains containing registered trademarks without the need to file a full lawsuit. With a trademark registration, these procedures are simple and cost effective. Without a registration, they become costly and more complicated, or may not be available.

Google AdWords: Buy a Competitor's Trademark to Divert Customers

In many industries today, business owners purchase keywords for paid search engine results. A common, unscrupulous practice occurs when a company purchases the trademark of a competitor from Google and uses it to advertise his or her services. This practice diverts traffic away from the trademark owner and increases the price the trademark owner must pay to use their trademarks in paid search marketing. *How does this happen?*

The brand owner purchasing its own trademarks for paid search marketing is being forced to bid against a competitor for use of their own trademark in a keyword ad campaign. Alphabet (formerly known as Google) loves selling to the highest bidder since competitive bidding drives up the cost to purchase AdWords, including trademarks. A registered trademark is a tool to force competitors to cease this practice when it is discovered.

Alphabet has been sued countless times over the practice. However, Alphabet has outspent every business who has tried to stop the practice, including American Airlines. Because of their deep pockets, the company has been able to sidestep a ruling as to its own direct liability for the sale of the trademarks. As a result, and as a practical matter, the owners of trademarks that are auctioned off to the owner's competitors must go after the competitor directly. A registered trademark is a vital tool to do so.

Social Media Squatters and ISP Takedown

Theft of trademarks on Facebook, Instagram, and other social media platforms is also an everyday occurrence. While social media platforms have complaint procedures, the chances of stopping an infringing use are not good unless you have a registered trademark since the platforms require proof of trademark rights before they will act to remove an infringing name.

Online Market Places

Thousands of brands sell goods and services via online market places such as Amazon, Etsy, and Alibaba. Amazon has created the Amazon Brand Registry to validate rights in brand names of products sold on Amazon. The brand owner must have an active trademark registration and be able to verify the owner's identity. Amazon now verifies the brand name being used by means of a code sent to the trademark representative listed at the U.S. Trademark Office.

Amazon promises that upon enrollment, the Brand Registry will give you greater influence and control over your product listings on Amazon, powerful search tools, and proactive brand protection to remove suspected infringing or inaccurate content. Alibaba, the Chinese version of Amazon, has even announced its plans to help smaller U.S. brands expand internationally by providing them access to its huge international marketplace. As U.S. brands expand through these channels, registered trademarks become an even more important tool to vaccinate your brand against online poachers.

Counterfeit Goods

Millions of products are sold on sites like eBay, Amazon, and Alibaba. Most products are authentic. Many are not. The latter are the proverbial "Chinese carbon copy." The world of counterfeit goods, both online and off, is growing daily. A registered trademark helps with both of these threats.

First, trademark registrations can be listed with U.S. Customs and Border Protection to prevent fake goods from being imported into the United States. Counterfeits can be identified by customs officials and stopped from entering the country.

Registrations also assist with efforts to have counterfeit goods removed from Alibaba, eBay, and Amazon. Like social media complaint mechanisms, a registered trademark is considered a prerequisite to obtaining cooperation from the large shopping sites where online "stores" post their own product listings.

The Right to Expand into New Territories and Sell Related Goods

A U.S. trademark registration is national in scope, regardless of the actual geographic use of the mark. A federal registration allows the owner time to expand into new states and territories even if the products or services have not yet been sold in the fifty states.

U.S. registrations also serve as the basis for applying for a registration in foreign countries. To learn more about foreign registration read: *Trademark Registration Goes Global.*[1]

Registration also allows a brand owner to develop new products that, although not identical, are related to those described in the registration. Related goods are products that are used together or that consumers assume emanate

---

1   Trademark Registration Goes Global:
https://brandaide.com/international-trademark-registration-2/

from the same source. Examples are vodka and orange juice and peanut butter and jam.

Not all words or phrases qualify for registration. Selection of a strong name is an important first step. In Chapter Two, you will learn the types of marks and which qualify for a registered trademark. An understanding of what can and cannot be registered is foundational. Step one of our three steps is "Select." **Select** a mark that intersects with legal protection, since it's a huge waste of time and money to seek registration for terms that will be rejected out of hand.

Select. Secure. Sustain.™

FIVE CHOICES
FOR A TRADEMARK

Two Are Really Bad

WHEN TRADEMARK SELECTION MEETS LEGAL PROTECTION, IT WILL BE A GREAT MARRIAGE

A STRONG TRADEMARK IS VITAL to the brand building process. When selecting a trademark to marry to your brand values and message, it's important to know whether your chosen name can be legally registered and enforced against third party users in the market. The ability to protect your mark should inform your final trademark selection.

As we noted early on, a brand name or design is capable of being protected only if it is distinctive. A brand is distinctive and protectable if is either 1) inherently distinctive; or 2) has acquired distinctiveness as a result of extensive marketing and advertising, often called "secondary meaning."

Before filing an application to register, an important step in your prefiling plan is to review and categorize your selection. Knowing whether your chosen name can be legally protected and registered *before* making a final selection is essential. Understanding where a proposed mark lands on the "trademark continuum" can mean the difference between owning a valuable brand name that increases the bottom line and owning a worthless descriptive or generic term that cannot function as a trademark. Don't waste time or precious resources filing for a worthless name, an all too common mistake.

WHAT IS THE TRADEMARK CONTINUUM?

The trademark continuum is a framework used by brand protection professionals as well as courts to determine the degree of protection afforded to any given term. The strength (and hence, degree) of legal protection is based on a series of labels: *coined (also known as fanciful), arbitrary, suggestive, descriptive,* and *generic.* The first three categories of marks are considered *inherently distinctive*, meaning they are great trademarks and can be registered and enforced with no additional legal burden of proof. The last two, descriptive and generic, should be avoided.

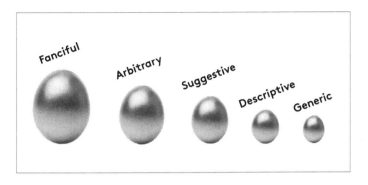

The Trademark Continuum
The stronger the mark, the greater the value.

Greater risks and increased legal and marketing costs are associated with a weak selection. Conversely, the larger the egg, as shown in our series of golden eggs above, the greater the potential for increased brand value—and the less you will pay to protect and enforce the mark over the long term.

> 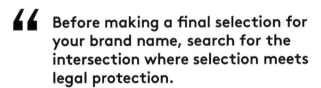 **Before making a final selection for your brand name, search for the intersection where selection meets legal protection.**

Some terms fit neatly into a clear category, others are more difficult to analyze and fall into the high-risk category. The further down the continuum one moves, the less protection courts afford to the brand name. For example, if a mark is descriptive, the owner will be unable to stop third parties from using the mark unless the brand owner can also gather and produce expensive evidence that proves to a court that consumers recognize the mark as being associated with your goods and services. This is a costly process few trademark owners can afford to engage in, yet one that is easily avoidable. The owner of a descriptive mark must pay multiple six figures to gather survey evidence just to prove the public recognizes the term as a trademark. Don't go down that fork in the road! Simply choose a strong, legally protectable mark from the outset.

Keep in mind that some marks are a matter of subjective interpretation by both attorneys and even judges. For this reason, if you have any doubts, make certain to obtain advice from a qualified professional before making a final selection or before crossing one off the list. We'll soon review an example of a strong suggestive mark that an attorney (not me) told my client was not registerable when in fact it was a great suggestive mark, capable of full legal protection. Let's review some examples of each.

THE TYPES OF MARKS AND WHERE THEY LAND ON THE CONTINUUM

Coined (also known as Fanciful)

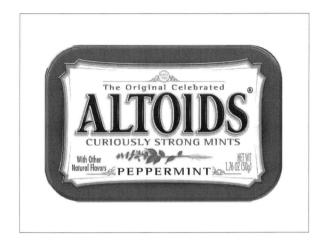

Coined, or fanciful marks, are terms that are conjured up to function as trademarks. The name does not exist prior to your creating it. Coined marks are inherently distinctive and therefore entitled to the greatest degree of legal protection.

ALTOIDS® is one of the oldest trademarks still in use, first used in the nineteenth century! No wonder it is known by its tagline (which is also a strong mark): *"The Original Celebrated Curiously Strong Peppermint."*

Another well-known coined mark is **Xerox®**. Xerox was created from the word *xerography,* a Greek term meaning dry writing. Chester Carlson was a patent attorney who was smart enough to know he needed a very strong trademark.

He went out and created one. Xerox is such a great example because the founder also created the generic term to go with the trademark: "the photocopy machine."

When one launches a new revolutionary product like the photocopier, it is especially important to manage and educate the consumer as to the proper use of your trademark from the beginning. Without, there is the risk the trademark can become identified as the generic term or name of the product and lose its protection as a trademark. When this happens, the brand is now in the public and is free for anyone to use. The trademark graveyard is filled with now generic terms that were once coined marks that were allowed to fall into the public domain. Former trademarks that became generic, such as cellophane, aspirin, and escalator, are now in the public vernacular, free for all to use.

Arbitrary

An everyday word, picture, or symbol in common use can be applied in an arbitrary manner to goods and services that are unrelated to the term being used as a mark. This results in a strong mark. Apple® and the famous bitten apple logo are arguably the world's strongest arbitrary marks.

Other well-known examples are DIESEL for clothing, and BLACK FLAG for entertainment services.

Diesel for a car engine is generic, but the same word becomes a strong arbitrary mark when used for a brand of clothing. Apple for a fruit is generic, but when applied to music or computers, it is a strong arbitrary mark.

Suggestive

Terms that suggest but do not describe the qualities, ingredients, or characteristics of a product are great marks, if you can create one! A suggestive mark is inherently distinctive, one of the strongest marks of all. Selection of a suggestive mark can be tricky because there is often a fine line between a descriptive and suggestive mark which can be subject to two interpretations. If you land on the descriptive side, you end up in a different neighborhood where your selection is not registerable and extremely difficult to enforce against infringers. You are also more likely to encounter an examining attorney who does not understand the mark or the goods and services to which it is applied, and incorrectly rejects your application.

Selecting a distinctive suggestive mark is even more challenging for new brand owners who naturally gravitate toward descriptive terms. After all, they want customers to understand what the company is offering. However, describing the product or services offered under your brand is best left to advertising and marketing materials, not your brand name.

INTERIOR ALIGNMENT® is a *very* strong suggestive mark. When one sees or hears the mark, one wonders exactly what type of interior is being aligned. The viewer wonders what goods or services are being offered for sale by the owner.

INTERIOR ALIGNMENT was one of the rare 30 to 35 percent of all applications that are approved for registration *without any Trademark Office objection.* The application I filed *sailed* through the rigorous Trademark Office examination process without even a word. As such, it became one of only approximately 35 percent of all applications filed that are immediately approved for registration by the Trademark Office without the need to file a formal amendment or written response to rejections on legal grounds.

INTERIOR ALIGNMENT was finally registered years after the attorney that my client had originally consulted told her the term could not be registered. I reassured the client it was a strong mark and that she must file for the registration. Interior Alignment is now a strong, distinctive, and legally protected brand name for the art of Feng Shui.

 It is quite impossible to get any rule out of the cases beyond this: That the validity of the mark ends where suggestion ends and description begins.

Descriptive

By far, the most troublesome and often confusing area of deciding the strength of a mark is the suggestive/descriptive label, as is illustrated by the INTERIOR ALIGNMENT example and our little character on the tight rope.

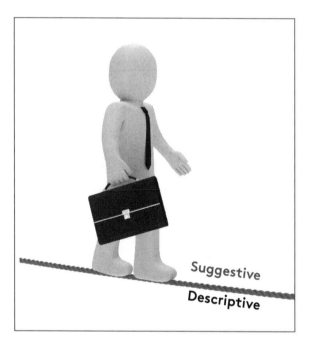

The previous quote is from Judge Learned Hand (what a name!) in a trademark legal opinion decided years ago. It is still true today. Whereas suggestive marks are strong and easily protected, descriptive terms are not. Nevertheless, courts often have trouble determining whether a particular mark is descriptive or suggestive. A descriptive mark is one that describes the intended purpose, function, or use of the goods. It can describe a class of users, the nature of the goods, the end effect upon the user, or a desirable characteristic of the goods and services.

The common test applied by courts to determine whether a given mark is suggestive or descriptive is the "imagination" test. The test was formulated by Judge Weinfeld in a 1968 New York trademark case.[2]

A term is suggestive if it requires imagination, thought, and perception to reach a conclusion as to the nature of the goods. A term is descriptive if it conveys an immediate idea of the ingredients, qualities, or characteristics of the goods. When evaluating your own proposed mark to decide if it is descriptive or suggestive, answer this question:

"How immediate and direct is the thought process to go from the designation to some characteristic of the product?"

If your customer or client needs to exercise mature thought or follow a multi-stage reasoning process to determine attributes of the product or service, then the term is suggestive, not descriptive. If this is the case, your mark is distinctive and can be registered with no problem. Most important, it can be protected against third parties who poach your mark. Interior Alignment is an example of this thought process.

---

2   *Stix Products, Inc. v. United Merchants & Mfrs.,* Inc., 295 F. Supp. 479, 488, 160 U.S.P.Q. 777 (S.D. N.Y. 1968)

Here are some examples of marks held to be suggestive when their owners went to court to enforce them:

- ➤ GLOW for skin cream

- ➤ ORACLE for computer software

- ➤ PENGUIN for food freezers

- ➤ SAMSON for weight training machines

Incongruity is also a strong indicator of suggestiveness. One of my personal favorites is the mark ROACH MOTEL for insect traps which was held suggestive for that reason. "[I]ts very incongruity is what catches one's attention."

If the brand name you select lands on the suggestive side, you've got a strong mark, like INTERIOR ALIGNMENT. If you fall into the descriptive abyss, watch out below, as you'll soon understand.

❞ The task of describing the product or services offered under your brand name is best left to advertising and marketing materials, not as part of your brand.

As previously discussed, descriptive terms may not be enforced as trademarks absent proof of acquired distinctiveness or secondary meaning, an additional legal requirement imposed upon descriptive terms as a condition of a grant of protection and enforcement against third parties using the same term.

Some of the most valuable advice I offer to a client is when I attempt to dissuade someone from selecting a descriptive term as a brand name. The speed bump looks minor, but it is a disguised pothole that can completely derail your brand and efforts to obtain a registered trademark, not to mention make enforcement costly and difficult.

 The more brands that use a common prefix or suffix, the weaker the mark, particularly where the prefix or suffix is descriptive.

Applications to register terms that are descriptive are rejected by the Trademark Office. In 2015, nearly 30,000 applications to register were rejected on grounds the marks sought to be registered were descriptive! While the Trademark Office may offer the owner to be listed on the Supplemental Register, there are few legal benefits to such a registration. **Read:** *Rehab for Bad Brands.*[3]

At the end of five years on the Supplemental Register, the owner can submit evidence that the mark has become distinctive and be allowed to move the registration to the Principal Register. However, in any later litigation the owner must still prove the mark has achieved popularity, and is recognized by consumers for the goods or services being offered to the public before a court will protect the mark!

This requires a costly uphill legal battle should the need arise to enforce the mark against third parties, all

---

3   *Rehab for Bad Brands:* https://brandaide.com/rehab-for-bad-brands/

before the owner even has the right to put on evidence against the infringer.

Two Descriptive Terms That Spent a Fortune Trying to Protect a Descriptive Mark

A few years ago, American Blinds® tried to sue Google for selling its trademark "American Blinds" as an AdWord to American's competitors. Google had the case thrown out because American Blinds was held descriptive despite years of advertising and use. The judge agreed with Google that American Blinds was descriptive and could not be protected. Despite years of use and advertising, and lots of money spent to prove the public knew the name, it was all for naught.

A more recent example of a costly legal battle and uncertain outcome facing owners of descriptive terms is demonstrated by Apple's battle to secure registration for iPAD.[4] Both parties to the action had a weak legal position, although Apple managed to squeak through and secure registration. The case is informative for new brand owners since the facts serve to illustrate several key principles.

Both Apple and its opposer RxD Media began with two strikes against each of them. While neither party had a strong legal position, Apple is the 1000-pound gorilla whose use in the market established secondary meaning that many young brands could never prove. Unless you are Apple, you won't have the resources to do so either!

---

4   *RxD Media, LLC v. IP Application Development LLC,* 125 USPQ2d 1801 (TTAB 2018)

Three strikes and you are out!" In this case, RxD Media managed to accumulate *five* strikes before the court finally kicked them off the field.

Strike 1: Weak prefixes in a mark in common use are not protectable. The letters "I" and "E" before a word as in iPad are commonly considered to refer to an Internet product or service.

Strike 2: The word "pad" was also descriptive for a "writing pad." Even Apple's application to register was initially refused by the Trademark Examiner, necessitating proof of secondary meaning in the market. Apple has the resources to achieve secondary meaning and pay the legal costs of proving they have done so. Emerging brands are not usually in that position.

After clearing that hurdle, Apple's application was approved and then published for opposition by third parties as part of the registration process. RxD Media, the opposer, had used iPAD as far back as 2007, but like our friend Mario, had never registered a trademark. It also had other serious issues that caused a complete strike out.

Strike 3: RxD never sought or received competent brand protection advice prior to the case or its evidence would have been much stronger. It might have even won the case! Its horrible trademark use and lack of samples to prove proper use were huge issues.

In the next chapter, we'll spend some time looking at building your own Brand Dream Team. Unfortunately, RxD had no team at all. Its only use of the term iPAD was as part of its compound mark that included a stylized pen followed by ".mobi" as shown here.

RxD was unable to establish a trademark identity for the word "iPAD" that was separate and apart from its stylized composite mark. The Court found RxD failed to establish an independent commercial impression upon the public for the words alone!

Strike 4: Because RxD had never filed for a registered trademark, it was not entitled to any of the statutory presumptions that accompany registration. Its case was based solely upon its common law use in the market. It faced an uphill battle and could not even show proper trademark use of the words.

Strike 5: You are out! Unlike Apple, RxD was also unable to show the mark was distinctive or had acquired distinctiveness. To the contrary, the evidence showed that RxD had been using the term in its advertising as a descriptive term. Oops. This is a perfect time to repeat the admonition about learning and following proper rules of trademark use. RxD clearly did not follow those rules. Have you ever heard an old expression, *"Be careful what you say and how you say it, or you may be hung by your own tongue"*? RxD largely hung itself by not taking care to vaccinate their brand!

As a post script, RxD has a new look and feel and, finally, a qualified trademark counsel. Below is a shot of their current trademark use. Note the logo is gone, and the word "ipad" is prominently displayed everywhere with a "TM." It's an example of "too little too late" or perhaps maybe "better late than never." While Apple can never stop them from using the name, since RxD was the first user, Apple owns the trademark registration and controls the marketplace. RxD failed to vax its brand name with a trademark registration that would have shut the door on Apple's efforts to register the name.

Generic

Generic terms are those words that *are* the name for the product. "Apple" for fruit is generic (but not for computers or iPhones). So is "Hotels.com" for hotels. Generic terms are *not trademarks* and will *never* be protected when applied to the goods or services they represent. Hotels. com has no rights to the word "hotels" because the site offers hotel reservations, which makes its term generic regarding the services offered.

Hotels.com

In summary, adoption and use of a descriptive term as a trademark leads to two problems that many owners can never overcome. First, registration is difficult if not impossible. And resulting registrations are often not worth the paper they are printed on. The owner operates under a somewhat delusional belief that a mark is protected and then learns otherwise when confronted with a problem in the marketplace.

Second, enforcement proceedings are more expensive and results less certain because the courts require a much higher standard of proof of acquired distinctiveness before granting protection. Opponents will exploit this weakness to its fullest.

❝ The moral of the story: Proper Selection and Protection are great bed fellows.

CREATE YOUR OWN BRAND DREAM TEAM

IN OUR PREVIOUS CHAPTER we learned that three of the five marks on the continuum are inherently distinctive and, if properly registered and sustained, will be afforded a strong level of protection by the law. Coined, Arbitrary, and Suggestive terms will be terrific brand ambassadors to communicate to your customer or audience. The remaining two are bad and should be avoided.

Words alone are not the only choices for brand ambassadors. The following are other types of marks that are commonly registered as trademarks:

➤ Words as a Phrase: slogan

➤ Letters and Words: a word or groupings of letters

➤ Personal Names used for specific goods and services and uncommon and rare surnames

- ➤ Logos: a design that becomes a mark when used in close association with the goods or services being marketed

- ➤ Trade Dress (requires proof of secondary meaning)

- ➤ Colors (requires proof of secondary meaning)

- ➤ Sound Marks (may require proof of secondary meaning)

WHAT MARKS ARE GOOD TEAM MEMBERS?

When selecting trademarks to serve as your brand messengers, consider assembling your own **brand dream team**. The typical brand dream team members include "the four horsemen" of a great brand:

- ✓ Words

- ✓ A logo

- ✓ A slogan

- ✓ A composite mark (words displayed in combination with a logo)

THE FOUR HORSEMEN OF A GREAT BRAND

The power of today's successful brand horsemen is akin to the horsepower found in a Ferrari. Given the speed with which communications happen in social media, viral marketing, and traditional media, brand dream team members must have the potential to circle the globe with the click of a mouse.

One of my favorite dream teams is the one created by Nike years ago, and which still serve to lead Nike products into the heart and minds, and onto the feet, of customers around the globe. A quick study of the Nike brand team will help you easily understand the members of the team and how they play alone as well as together in marketing the brand.

Nike is a wonderful example of the synergistic relationship between its marks and its values. That synergy results from the combination of products that customers love with a well-conceived and well-executed brand strategy. This iconic brand, launched by Phil Knight and Bill Bowerman in Portland in 1971, spawned a revolution in footwear for sports. It also created a global industry around that revolution. The famed Nike swoosh was designed by a Portland State University graphic design student, Carolyn Davidson.

Supporting a global empire that transcends all cultures, time, and space is a big task. Nike created a brand dream team that works. The team members are simple, distinctive, recognizable, and effective. They get the job done.

Together, the word Nike, its famous swoosh, and the slogan "Just Do It" form a composite mark. In this dancer ad, Nike has combined all three individual elements into a composite mark: the words, the famous swoosh, and the slogan. The brand team contains three individually protectable trademarks used alone or together to heighten brand recognition and communicate brand messages.

A brand dream team provides the words and symbols to which customers attach the meanings and attributes a company seeks to convey through marketing. A strong brand team multiplies marketing results, increases brand value over time, and strengthens legal protection.

The four horsemen must first be created and tested for messaging and perception. Next, in concert with a live brand team member, they must be vetted, analyzed, and thoughtfully protected. Are they up to the task? Are they strong? Are they protectable? Do they stand out in a crowd across multiple platforms of communication? Is the marketplace cluttered with many third-party uses? Unless your prospective team members pass these tests, they don't qualify for a spot on your dream team. Though these steps may sound obvious—and they are—many new brand owners overlook them.

Once your dream team has been carefully selected, screened, and properly secured by means of effective registration, the next step is to develop a plan to use them individually as well as together in marketing and advertising. Over time, with consistent use and repeated exposure, consumers will learn to recognize the four elements, whether they appear alone or together.

If they think your dreams are crazy,
show them what crazy dreams can do.

Just do it.

Nike's brand elements exemplify the perfect brand team. If Nike removes its name from its advertising, consumers nonetheless recognize it as a Nike advertisement. The Serena Williams ad shown above makes no mention of Nike at all, but for its swoosh and slogan appearing beneath the star of the ad, Serena Williams. The public recognizes this as a Nike ad even without the word mark even when the company displays only its swoosh or slogan.

The following are other examples that show how Nike mixes the elements.

The value of the Nike brand did not happen by accident. One could argue that although Nike began as one of the first running shoes, it has evolved into much more. Brand equity is the product of success in the market, as well as serious reflection during selection. Brand equity also results from consistent use and an ongoing program to protect and maintain the brand. Adoption and use of words and symbols without a clear plan or without proper analysis of the competitive landscape in which these messengers will operate can doom aspirations for brand value prior to first launch.

Compound Word Marks

Compound word marks are two or more distinct words that are represented as one word.

Here are some examples of famous compound word marks:

Composite (Combination) Mark

We've seen the Nike composite in several variations. Here are examples of composite marks that include current Wall Street darling NVIDIA. Nvidia makes the chips that go into video gaming consoles and our tech-laden new cars, to name but a few of their markets.

The composite mark combines elements that are often registered individually as well as in composite form.

Slogans

Slogans are a brief attention-getting phrase used in advertising or promotion. Here are some familiar and famous examples.

ALTOIDS
"The Curiously Strong Mints."

NIKE
"Just Do It."

SUBWAY
"Eat Fresh."

SKITTLES
"Taste the Rainbow."

Caveat: Registration will be refused if the slogan describes the services.

You will want to put your proposed slogans through the distinctive/generic test just as you have done for your word marks. I just love the ALTOIDS slogan, since if you look carefully you can learn how one brand turned an otherwise descriptive slogan into a masterful one that has served as one of the world's oldest trademarks.

Were the phrase "The Original Strong Mints," the slogan would have been descriptive and unregisterable. Someone cleverly made the phrase distinctive by the addition of two words. The additions of these out-of-character attributes transformed a descriptive slogan into a distinctive one. Mints may be strong, but they are not typically "celebrated," or "curiously strong."

Color as a Trademark

Color marks consist solely of one or more colors used on particular objects. Color is not easily registerable, but those who succeed are typically aggressive in protecting it. Here are two famous examples that have been successfully registered.

UPS
Big Brown Truck®
(This truck is brown.)

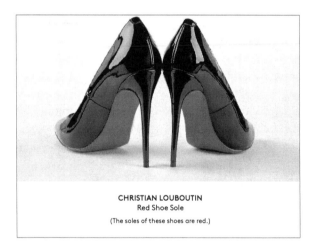

CHRISTIAN LOUBOUTIN
Red Shoe Sole
(The soles of these shoes are red.)

Protecting color is not for everyone, but who doesn't recognize the big brown truck even from a distance without words? And what woman doesn't love a red sole shoe from Christian Louboutin? I know I do!

Trade Dress

Can you spot the registered trademark in this photo?
The trademark is the lay out and design of the Apple store,
which is a registered trademark owned by Apple.

Trade dress is a distinctive shape, product configuration, or nonfunctional feature that acts like a trademark. Trade dress serves to identify the product or service, just as a word or phrase does. The star atop the Mont Blanc pen is considered trade dress. The layout and design of a restaurant has been approved as a trademark, and of course, the layout and design of the Apple store, are all examples of trade dress that have been registered as trademarks. Trademark registration for trade dress requires proof of secondary meaning. Here are a couple of other famous examples that have been registered for years:

Shape of the Coca-Cola Bottle

Adidas Stripes

Once you have selected your word mark and any logos, slogans, colors, or trade dress that might also qualify, filing a trademark application is the next step. See Chapter 5.

Before moving on to our next chapter, go to **https//:brandaide.com/vaxplan** and complete the next part of the SELECT section. List any additional marks you might want on your own brand dream team.

In the next chapter, you will learn about The Brand Called You. The personal brand needs to be nurtured and protected, much like that for a product or service.

THE BRAND CALLED YOU

THE NOTION OF PERSONAL BRANDING was popularized after Tom Peters's article, "The Brand Called You," appeared in *Fast Company* in 1997.

> **It's time for me—and you—to take a lesson from the big brands, a lesson that's true for anyone who's interested in what it takes to stand out and prosper in the new world of work.**
>
> **Regardless of age, regardless of position, regardless of the business we happen to be in, all of us need to understand the importance of branding. We are CEOs of our own companies: Me Inc. To be in business today, our most important job is to be head marketer for the brand called You.**
>
> **—TOM PETERS**

Whether Peters's article launched the personal branding trend or simply exposed an already unfolding phenomenon is unclear. However, as Peters keenly stated: "The Web makes the case for branding more directly than any packaged good or consumer product ever could. Here's what the Web says: Anyone can have a website."

Personal branding is the practice of marketing oneself and one's career or some aspect as a brand and protecting it through registered trademarks. Personal branding is often discussed in the context of the ongoing process of establishing a prescribed image or impression in the mind of others about an individual or group.

Celebrities such as performers, actors, and well-known athletes are the first to come to mind when one thinks of the personal brand. Public figures are typically highly paid in their professions, and often garner even greater income from endorsements of products and services, or creating their own branded product or service. The celebrity often protects his or her personal name by means of a series of registered trademarks.

❝ Everybody will be world famous for fifteen minutes.

— ANDY WARHOL

Andy Warhol, the famed '60s pop artist and self-created brand is an early example of how the individual celebrity and personal brands intersect. Warhol understood this more than any artist of his generation. His art was famous, but he was the celebrity.

The topic of personal branding has now expanded from the red carpets of Hollywood to the corridors of Wall Street and Main Street. Social media influencers are now highly paid celebrities. There are books, seminars, workshops, and trainings on how to lead a workshop on the topic of personal branding.

Personal branding for professionals is a profession unto itself. Personal branding is now a topic among service professionals who must now learn to market their services both online and off. Doctors, attorneys, real estate professionals, and accountants, to name but a few, attend workshops and seminars on the topic. Writers opine on the topic with regularity: *The Definitive Guide to Personal Branding,*[5] *The Complete Guide to Building Your Personal Brand,*[6] and *10 Golden Rules of Personal Branding.*[7]

Individuals with a large Internet following, as well as performers, actors, and athletes are typically more vulnerable to online infringements by cyber squatters and opportunists. Individual celebrity names for products, services, and the products they endorse are typically well represented and protected for this reason. They serve as a model for other service professionals in a niche or specialty.

Many individuals have achieved prominence within their specialty. Thousands of people are now developing online businesses using their expertise to coach and train others. They are able to achieve a global audience by means of live events attracting attendees from around the globe, as well as online marketing events including webinars, product launches, and social media followings.

Registered trademarks are but one vehicle for protecting live and online trainings, workshops, seminars, and certification programs. Registration can be secured for a number of different goods and services, including workshops, online trainings, a series of books with the same title, audio and video recordings, and websites providing content to clients and the public at large.

---

5   *The Definitive Guide to Personal Branding,* https://brandyourself.com/definitive-guide-to-personal-branding

6   *The Complete Guide to Building Your Personal Brand,* https://www.quicksprout.com/the-complete-guide-to-building-your-personal-brand/

7   *10 Golden Rules of Personal Branding, Forbes,* https://www.forbes.com/sites/goldiechan/2018/11/08/10-golden-rules-personal-branding

Many of these professionals go on to offer advanced certification and "train the trainer" programs that establish their legacy. The registered trademark that identifies these programs becomes the foundation of a sustainable legacy brand.

Individuals with certification programs are legally required under trademark law to have written license agreements with users of the brand. The written license must include the right to exercise quality control. The owner of any trademark must control the quality of the offerings under their brand names, lest they be lost.

Without a written trademark license, certification marks are vulnerable to loss when third parties who have not been licensed attempt to trade off the reputation and hard work of those who have invested to train in the specific modality or service offering. The founder of the training and sole owner of the mark used by the licensees must protect the trademark against outside poachers for the benefit of all those who are licensed to use the mark after completing certification.

A REGISTERED TRADEMARK HELPS YOU SLEEP BETTER

Of course a registered trademark is not an approved sleep aid, but now that you know the risks to your business if you do not have one, you may well rest easier knowing you are protected. What if you woke up and, logged on, and your site had disappeared? Or, you learn there is now a replica of your site in the Netherlands offering your same training certification program in Dutch? Or, you are featured as an author in a "book" composed of chapters stolen from books of different authors, implying you agreed to participate and contribute your material? These are examples of some of my clients' experiences.

A registered trademark won't stop online thieves, but it will provide a potent, inexpensive tool with which to deal with online poachers swiftly, and with the least expense possible. Conversely, without the protection afforded by a registration, and should you need to go after an infringer, it will be the legal equivalent of being forced to slog uphill in the snow with your skis on. Which option sounds better?

Here are some of the common Internet violations that plague the personal brand owner:

1. Registration and use of his or her name in a domain name without consent.

2. Use of an individual's name or likeness on a site to market someone else's products either directly or through purchase of the individual's name as a sponsored ad word.

3. Use of the individual's name or creative work to create a false "implied endorsement."

A registered trademark helps to combat these issues while maintaining strength and integrity.

A registration for a personal name establishes the individual's name as a legally protected brand for the goods and services which are sold under the personal name. The registration provides easy access to remedies for common Internet crimes that arise, including cybersquatting and online trademark infringement. Finally, a registration supplements non-trademark rights, such as the right of publicity, which is most useful in cases where an individual's name or likeness is used in connection with the sale of a product or service.

HOW DOES A FEDERAL TRADEMARK BENEFIT THE INDIVIDUAL?

All brands, including individuals with an online following, are particularly vulnerable to brandjacking. "Brandjacking" is "to hijack a brand to deceive or divert attention; often used in abusive or fraudulent activities devised for gain at the expense of the goodwill, brand equity and customer trust of actual brand owners."[8]

Let's review the common types of brandjacking the personal brand encounters.

Unauthorized Use of an Individual's Name in a Domain Name

What happens when an individual's name (or your product brand) ends up in the URL of a domain owned and used by a third party?

---

8   *Mark Monitor, Glossary* 2008, https://www.markmonitor.com/new-gtld-resource-center/new-gtld-resources/new-gtld-glossary/

An individual whose name has been unlawfully registered and used in a domain may file an action to recover ownership of the infringing domain with the World Intellectual Property Organization (WIPO) or the National Arbitration Forum, using the *Uniform Domain Dispute Resolution Proceeding* ("UDRP").

The UDRP was created as an alternative to costly federal court litigation, and provides a streamlined procedure to secure return of the domain regardless of where the registrant is living. You can recover a domain from a resident of China as easily as from one in Africa or the U.S. When you register a domain through an ICANN (The Internet Corporation for Assigned Names and Numbers) affiliated registrar, as a condition of the registration, the registrant must consent to the jurisdiction of an ICANN approved arbitration panel to decide disputes over ownership of domains containing trademark rights of others. Costs are substantially less than a court proceeding because all proceedings are in writing.

You will be required to prove three elements to secure return of the domain:

➤ The disputed domain name is identical or confusingly similar to a trademark or service mark in which the Complainant has rights;

➤ The registrant has no legitimate rights in the mark; and

➤ Registration was made in bad faith.

➤ The first element is proven by proving ownership of a registered trademark. In a decision
involving the domain sylviabrownehypnosis.
com[9], the UDRP Panel stated: "In line with
countless prior UDRP panels, the Panel finds
such evidence [of a federal registration] sufficient to establish the Complainant's rights
in its mark." In short, a federal registration is
automatic proof of the first element, which
eliminates requiring further proof of use of the
mark as a trademark for goods and services.

Contrast this decision with cases in which a well-known
person without a trademark registration is unsuccessful in
recovering the domain because he or she cannot prove
common law trademark rights. David Pecker, an individual in the news as of late, offers an amusing example of a
famous person who could not prove trademark rights in
his name.

DAVID PECKER AND A PORN SITE

While David Pecker was not a household name, he has
been well-known in media circles as the Chairman and CEO
of American Media, Inc., owner of such notables as the
National Enquirer and *Star.* Over his 35-year career, Pecker
completed more than $3.6 billion in magazine transactions
and is most recently known for his practice of "catch and

9   *Sylvia Browne Corp. v. Younghee Kim,* WIPO Case No. D2007-1715.

kill" at the *National Enquirer,* namely purchasing negative stories about President Trump and "killing the story" to prevent negative public exposure.

In 2006, Mr. Pecker attempted to recover the domain "www.davidpecker.com" from a California man who registered the domain and populated a landing page with links to various porn sites. The arbitration panel rejected Mr. Pecker's claim to the domain on grounds that Pecker had provided no evidence proving he had trademark rights in the name.

Mr. Pecker's case is but one of thousands of instances where individuals have been forced to seek relief to prevent use of their personal names and brands in unflattering or deceptive ways. Unlike Mr. Pecker, for those individuals providing online products and services using their personal brand name, it makes sense to be armed with a federal registration. The registered trademark is like a vaccination for your brand, a Brand Vax.

The test articulated by WIPO is whether the individual's name has been used for trade or commerce, or whether the Complainant had *"ever used his personal name for the purpose of advertising or promoting his business or for the sale of any goods or services."* Mr. Pecker was unable to meet the standard of proof required to protect his own name.

These examples serve to emphasize the importance of a federal registration to recapture both domains stolen by hijackers, as well registrations containing your mark and used to promote competitive goods and services. The UDRP provides a short cut to avoid the results obtained by Mr. Pecker.

Are you using your personal name to sell a product or service? Or, have you endorsed a product or service, or granted rights to others to use your name to market or promote a product or service? If so, go to **https://brandaide.com/vaxplan** before proceeding to Chapter Five.

Now that you understand how a registered trademark acts to immunize your brand from brandjacking online, let's get to the process of how it all happens. In the next chapter, you'll learn about the actual process involved in securing a registered trademark.

In Chapter Five, we move on to Step Two, SECURE your brand by filing to register members of your brand dream team.

THE TRADEMARK APPLICATION PROCESS

STEP TWO: SECURE YOUR BRAND (a.k.a. VAX YOUR BRAND BY EXECUTING YOUR PLAN)

NOW THAT YOU HAVE SELECTED YOUR MARKS—which we know will be protectable (right?)—and decided who will play on your team, how do you finally secure them via a registered trademark? In this chapter you will learn the process of applying for a registration and doorways in which you can enter to successfully register.

There are three doorways from which one can enter the trademark registration process. These doors are the filing basis set forth in the trademark law. Each lead to the same destination but take a different procedural route.

HOW THE TRADEMARK REGISTRATION PROCESS WORKS

There are three ways to file to register a U.S. trademark:

➤ Intent to Use

➤ Actual Use

➤ Based upon a foreign application or existing registration

Regardless of which filing route you choose, the examination process is exactly the same. The only difference is when the application is based on Intent to Use, the owner is not required to submit samples with the initial application. Samples showing use of the mark are sent later, after the product is first sold or the services performed.

Intent to Use

If you are a startup or have developed a new product but have not yet started selling it, you can "reserve" your trademark in advance of the first actual sale of your product or offering of your services.

Even if approved, the registration will not be issued until you actually sell the products or offer the services and file to show that use has begun. There is an additional fee to file the proof of use.

An Intent to Use (ITU) application is an invaluable tool with which to vaccinate your brand names prior to launch and public exposure to others. By filing an ITU application (and assuming you've done your homework to select a distinctive mark and cleared its availability), you will have time to develop marketing and packaging and to finalize manufacturing for products without the risk that someone else will beat you to the Trademark Office. Even though your registration won't issue until *after* you launch your product or service, your *prior pending* application will act as a bar to prevent later-filed applications for the same or similar mark from proceeding to registration prior to yours.

I have certainly seen clients who waited to file and found out later that someone else beat them to the punch. Third parties can get the same ideas by coincidence, more often than a deliberate taking. Remember ideas are floating out there, free for anyone to use and appropriate. Until you apply to register a word or phrase for specific goods or services, they are just that, ideas free for anyone to use. Keep in mind that trademark filings are public record, so if secrecy about the launch of a new product is a concern, filing as soon as use is established may be a better choice.

Actual Use

When your trademark is already in use, *i.e.,* you are selling goods or services under the mark in commerce prior to the date of filing, you should file based upon use in commerce. If your company has been selling a product but never registered the brand name, then you will file the application with proof of use and proceed directly to registration, (provided there are no prior registrations that would block your application, or the mark is not descriptive or generic).

Based Upon a Foreign Registration

Trademark owners with a pending application or existing registration in a foreign country can base a U.S. registration upon the pending application and any foreign registration that issues. This is an extremely tricky area of the law, since the international trademark treaties permit one to file a foreign application based upon the home country application within six months of the original application, and still receive the same priority date as the first home country filing.

There have been instances in which my client filed in the U.S. first, or so we thought, only to find out later in the process that a foreign application had been filed several months prior to our U.S. application. That foreign owner then filed in the U.S. *after* our filing date but was able to claim priority over my clients' applications. This simply means the filing date in the U.S. is deemed to be the same date of the foreign application, even though it was actually filed months later. Note, that the reverse is equally true.

When you file into a foreign country based upon your U.S. application, you will receive the same filing date as that of your U.S. application, if your foreign application is filed within six months of your U.S. application. Keep this in mind if you will be marketing overseas or have a foreign licensee or distributor, making a foreign registration important.

Another pitfall for U.S. owners is foreign registrations containing broad claims for rights in goods and services that are not being sold by the trademark owner. When using a foreign application or registration as a basis for filing, the foreign applicant need not prove use in the U.S., but instead is able to rely solely upon the items registered in their home country. This is a rare loophole in U.S. law, again based upon international treaties. Unlike the U.S., most of the rest of the world does *not* require proof of actual use of a mark prior to registration.

Most, if not all, U.S. applications by foreign owners involve overly broad claims for many goods and services within a given category. Since the treaties require that each member country give full recognition to registrations lawfully issued in the home country, the U.S. allows the same goods and services to be registered in the U.S. without proof of use. For the first six years following registration, those descriptions will block U.S. applicants who have lawful prior use for the same goods and services!

The Examination Process

As we learned earlier, approximately *67 percent* of all U.S. trademark applications receive a refusal to register. Given these odds, you can now see the import of good planning before filing. Advance planning reduces the odds of a fatal defect in your filing that will completely prevent registration.

Each trademark application is assigned to an attorney in the Trademark Office. Within four to six months after your filling, the assigned Examiner reviews the application to determine whether it meets the filing and legal requirements. The application is reviewed to verify a claim of ownership, what goods and services you are claiming, in what categories they belong, the manner of use in advertising and on the goods, the description of goods or services, and whether the samples of use are acceptable. Certain defects cannot be remedied, in which case registration will be refused.

The Examiner issues an Office Action, which must be answered within six months from the date it is issued, or the application is abandoned and lost. An important key to successful trademark registration is filing the initial application correctly. This includes knowing **what and how to file**, based on a strategy that maximizes the chances of success. Knowing what variation of a mark to file for, as well as what goods and services should be claimed and how to describe them requires significant experience since. If the application is filed incorrectly, many errors cannot be corrected. The application will be lost.

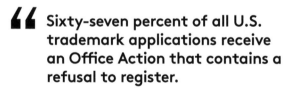 **Sixty-seven percent of all U.S. trademark applications receive an Office Action that contains a refusal to register.**

The Examiner will evaluate whether the proposed trademark is distinctive and not descriptive. This is by far the biggest problem new brand owners have in understanding trademarks. A mark that describes the goods or services, or even a quality or ingredient of the goods or services, cannot be registered. Marks that are scandalous or which are geographically descriptive will also be refused registration.

Examiners can be wrong on these issues. As a result, a descriptive refusal is one for which you will most certainly need proven expertise to respond and overcome the rejection. Examiners are helpful but they are not there to provide free legal advice to applicants. For these reasons, it is important to know prior to filing whether you have selected a descriptive term incapable of being successfully registered. If you have made time to select wisely, then you and your counsel will be better prepared to successfully respond to the Examiner's refusal to register when it arrives, and it likely will. It bears repeating: **Why waste valuable time and money trying to register the two bad choices?** Kick them to the curb in exchange for one of the three good ones! Choose a mark that can be protected and is not diluted by multiple uses of a common word, prefix, or suffix in your industry.

Other common problems are procedural, such as when the drawing does not match the samples of use submitted, the description of a mark is incorrectly worded, or the goods and services are improperly classified.

Next, the Trademark Examiner reviews pending and existing federal registrations to decide if there is an earlier filed application or existing registration that is confusingly similar. Other marks need not be identical to cause yours to be rejected. In fact, most are not and may include a common word, prefix, or other element, or are registered for nonidentical, but *related* goods. Like a rejection based upon descriptiveness, the related goods refusal is common and often difficult to overcome without expertise in the field. Deciding if goods or services are related can be quite complex.

Once approved, the application is published publicly for opposition. Any other brand owner, or anyone who feels they could be damaged to file an opposition to prevent registration. If no one opposes within 30 days from the date of publication, the registration will normally issue a few weeks thereafter.

Since the odds of a rejection are so high, in our next chapter we will review the most common objections you are likely to encounter. By knowing them ahead of time, you'll be able to sidestep them in advance.

AVOID THE PAIN OF REJECTION

Common Reasons Applications Are Refused

BEFORE YOU ARE READY TO FILE, there are three important prefiling steps to complete in your plan.

1. Search the market to avoid rejection based upon an existing application or registration for the same or related goods or services.

2. Establish proper trademark use of your marks in marketing and advertising that meets federal regulations.

3. Create a budget and manageable timeline to file applications to protect the brand dream team.

You will have the chance to complete these steps at the end of this chapter. But first, we'll briefly review the causes for rejection and how to avoid them. Once we've reviewed them, you'll be ready to make sure you are prepared to avoid them yourself.

(1)
LIKELIHOOD OF CONFUSION
WITH PENDING APPLICATIONS
OR REGISTRATIONS

The rules for determining confusion with another trademark fill volumes of legal decisions. The law can be confusing, and the case decisions contradictory. This is because there is a degree of subjectivity involved in making these decisions.

The important thing to remember is that two marks need not be identical to be considered confusing if they are used for the same goods or services. Equally important, goods and services need not be exactly the same as those in an existing registration to be considered confusing. It is sufficient if the goods and services are related, if the types of customers are the same, and if all or a portion of the marks are similar. Refusals to register based upon related goods or services are common. In my experience, these are the most complicated and difficult objections to overcome since the Examiner's opinion is subjective and not always valid. Yet, the evidence that can be submitted to overcome the refusal is limited. This is another reason a prior search is invaluable, since you are much more likely to anticipate related goods in the market if you have performed a search prior to filing.

❝ Failure to perform a trademark search is much like walking into a dark and crowded room without turning on the lights. You are likely to trip over someone or something.

Do you typically walk into a dark room without turning on the lights? Of course not. You'd be likely to trip over furniture in the room.

New brand owners often file for a trademark application without performing a search. When you neglect to perform a proper search prior to filing, it is akin to entering a dark room without turning on the lights to see who or what is there. When you fail to properly search before filing, you are relying upon the Trademark Office to decide if an existing registration or pending application will block yours. However, even a search of the U.S. Trademark Office does not disclose registrations in all of the 50 states, trade directories, phone books, and domain names. This is why launching use without a search is not a good idea. Read more: *A Trademark Search Is Important.*[10]

Go to **https://brandaide.com/vaxplan** to complete Part 1 of Step 2, Search.

---

10   *A Trademark Search Is Important:* https://brandaide.com/trademark-search-important

(2)
FAILURE TO PROVE
TRADEMARK USE

An all too common reason the Trademark Office refuses registration is because the owner cannot prove the term has been used as a trademark. This means the use in advertising must meet federal regulations (and there are hundreds of pages of them). If your use does not meet the technical and sometimes confusing rules issued by the Trademark Office, your application will be rejected.

 Make certain your marketing and advertising teams understand the rules of proper use and/or have your materials reviewed by counsel prior to final printing or manufacturing.

Correct use of a trademark is the manner in which the trademark owner, as well as third parties (including the media), present a brand name to the public. All marketing materials should present a clear, consistent presentation of the trademark. Where appropriate also include the identity of the generic product being offered for sale with a vision that is clearly communicated to prospective purchasers.

Example: BEN & JERRY'S ice cream

The Basics of Trademark Use

Trademarks should be used as an adjective and presented in a distinctive font. If the generic term for the product in included in marketing materials, present it in a smaller less distinctive font. This Peet's display is an example of proper use.

Another common mistake that reduces the strength of protection is when the mark sought to be registered includes the generic term as part of the mark. In the above BEN & JERRY'S example, the word ice cream is *not included in the trademark filing.* Trademark regulations state:

> **If a mark is comprised in part of matter that, as applied to the goods or services, is generic or does not function as a mark, the matter must be disclaimed to permit registration on the Principal Register.**

In short, this means, the generic term for the product is not protectable anyway, so why put it into the description of the mark, only to have to disclaim rights in it? Including the generic term actually narrows the scope of protection and can limit the ability to extend the mark to new products and services. Let's go back to the Amazon example. When Amazon first launched about the same time as Mario, Amazon was *only* an online bookseller. Had it registered AMAZON BOOKS, it would have been more difficult to expand into selling other items without a new registration for each item.

FRUIT OF THE LOOM may sell underwear. However, its registered trademark is *not* FRUIT OF THE LOOM UNDERWEAR, nor did Nike register NIKE RUNNING SHOES.

Another troublesome trend in recent years is when marketing and advertising teams insist on using a trademark in an all lowercase font, blending what should stand out into a sentence or surrounding text. This is a classic example of improper trademark use that is almost certain to trigger a refusal to register.

Use the Mark to Sell Specific Goods and Services

Because a trademark is designed to identify the source of goods and services, trademark law requires that the mark be used for the *sale* of those goods and services—it does not protect information about the product or service. You must prove you are actually selling the product or providing the service to the public. Trademark Office lawyers have the Internet too. The Examiner will review your website and search the Internet. If you have not used the term to actually sell goods and services, trademark registration will not be allowed. All advertising materials, packaging, and point-of-sale displays must clearly show that the mark is used to identify specific goods or services. Another common mistake by new brand owners is using a mark in a descriptive sense—as a trade name or corporate name, as part of a sentence or a press release—but failing to connect the term to the specific goods and services.

It bears repeating: trademarks must appear on the packaging or containers, or be clearly shown in a display of the goods. This means that the mark must appear either on the product itself, the packaging for the product, or the point-of-sale displays.

Special Rules Apply to Internet Trademark Use

When it comes to establishing trademark rights by means of Internet use, there are technical rules issued by the Trademark Office which govern electronic displays. The trademark must be used in an online display in close proximity to the goods or services. The brand names must appear in a distinctive font, in close proximity to the shopping cart or ordering page. For the detailed regulations on what's acceptable, it's best to review use of the mark with qualified counsel before launching. An experienced attorney will make certain your samples meet the regulations followed by the Trademark Examiners.

Improper Use Contributes to Loss of Rights

If the public begins using the trademark as the common name for the product, the mark is at risk to become generic. We refer to this as 'Genericide.'

Use the mark in a manner that will minimize the risk the mark will become generic or descriptive. A mark becomes generic (and no longer protectable as a trademark) when the public commonly uses the trademark as the generic name of the product. In other words, the trademark is absorbed into the common language. New, innovative products that achieve great success often face the greatest risk of becoming generic.

When you use "Xerox" the way you use "aspirin," we get a headache.
There's a new way to look at it.

Boy, what a headache! And all because some of you may be using our name in a generic manner. Which could cause it to lose its trademark status the way the name "aspirin" did years ago. So when you do use our name, please use it as an adjective to identify our products and services, e.g., Xerox copiers. Never as a verb: "to Xerox" in place of "to copy," or as a noun: "Xeroxes" in place of "copies." Thank you. Now, could you excuse us, we've got to lie down for a few minutes.

XEROX.

Remember these examples: cellophane, aspirin, and escalator? Although they began as trademarks, the public quickly adopted them as the generic term for the product Consequently, the trademarks were absorbed into the language. At that point, they were no longer protectable or enforceable as trademarks.

Genericide is often a result of the trademark owner's failure to police his or her mark against third parties. Designs and logos can also become generic. There is no better example than the "walking fingers" of the yellow pages. AT&T failed to police use of the mark by third parties, and a court held it had ceased to function as a trademark. Since its use was so widespread it had been lost all distinctiveness and could no longer function as a trademark.[11]

---

11   *Genericide, A Silent Killer:* https://brandaide.com/genericide/

In the next chapter, we'll look more closely at the need to police your registered trademarks in the marketplace.

Meanwhile, download the **FREE BRANDAIDE GUIDE TO TRADEMARK USE** at https://brandaide.com/guide-to-tm-use

Review this guide and your own trademark use on websites, in marketing materials, and in social media. Go to **https://brandaide.com/vaxplan** and complete Part 2 of Step 2.

(3)
WORDS THAT DESCRIBE GOODS OR SERVICES CANNOT BE REGISTERED

The entire purpose of a trademark is to distinguish goods and services, not to describe them. Words that describe are free for anyone to use, and they cannot be registered as a trademark without years of use and massive advertising expenditures to prove consumer recognition. To learn more read: *Rehab for Bad Brands.*[12]

Marketing teams love descriptive domain names and taglines that describe the product or service. As previously mentioned, the U.S. Trademark Office rejected almost 30,000 applications in one year on grounds they were descriptive! Leave descriptive and laudatory terms to your marketing materials and out of your brand name. To learn more read: *5 Choices for a Trademark and 2 are really Bad.*[13]

If you are uncertain, clear proposed marks with trademark counsel before adopting a mark. Don't rely upon marketing professionals or other nontrademark lawyers to give advice on whether a proposed brand name qualifies for trademark protection.

---

12   *Rehab for Bad Brands:* https://brandaide.com/rehab-for-bad-brands

13   *5 Choices for a Trademark and 2 Are Really Bad:* https://brandaide.com/5-choices-for-a-new-trademark-2-are-really-bad/

4

THE MARK YOU HAVE CHOSEN
IS PRIMARILY A SURNAME

Many brand names are often based upon the last name of the founder. The trademark statute prohibits registration of marks that are "primarily merely a surname." This is an extremely complicated area because there are exceptions, and each case is unique. There are specific factors that must be proven.

Surnames that are extremely rare and appear only a relatively few times in the U.S. Census are more likely to be registerable. If a name is so rare, it doesn't seem like a surname, it's more likely to be considered distinctive. For example, while PIRELLI for tires was held to have the look and feel of a surname, HACKLER did not. Evidence of whether the public would perceive the mark as a surname or as an arbitrary or fanciful term are also considered. Needless to say, if the proposed mark is a common surname like Smith or Jones, you can forget about registration as a trademark.

(5)

THE PROPOSED MARK IS PRIMARILY
GEOGRAPHICALLY DESCRIPTIVE

Every city and state in America is replete with local companies using a geographic identifier. Most are not registerable as trademarks. The rare ones are. If your mark contains a geographic term, and you receive a rejection, the Examiner in your case will need to prove three things:

(a) the primary significance of the mark is a generally known geographic location;

(b) the goods or services originate in the place identified in the mark; and

(c) purchasers would be likely to believe that the goods or services originate in the geographic place identified in the mark.

Examples:

➤ PARADISE ISLAND AIRLINES was found to be geographically descriptive since the airline flew to and from Paradise Island.

➤ CALIFORNIA PIZZA KITCHEN was found to be primarily geographically descriptive of restaurant services that originate in California.

But one of our favorite hot sauces made the cut:

✓ TAPATIO held not primarily geographically deceptively misdescriptive of hot sauce, despite the fact that the mark is a Spanish term meaning "of or pertaining to Guadalajara, Mexico" and the goods did not originate from Guadalajara.

If you are using a surname, or a geographic description, do secure professional advice before investing heavily in the name.

The last step before filing is to develop a budget for your protection. This is an important step to make sure your plan is implemented, even if it takes a year or more to do so. You'll need to include government filing costs based upon the goods and services you will be protecting, the number of team members you are filing to register, and whether you have launched or will be filing using Intent to Use. Finally, include professional fees if you are hiring an expert.

Go to **https://brandaide.com/vaxplan** to complete Part 3 of Step 2.

CONGRATULATIONS! YOU ARE APPROVED ... NOW WHAT?

> **A file cabinet is not a resort destination for your trademark registration. Monitoring your rights is a must!**

AFTER WAITING A YEAR OR LONGER, your application has been approved and registration has finally issued. Are you protected? Yes, *and* there is more work to be done. You must learn to monitor and police your rights lest your work be for naught.

A trademark registration is evidence of your right to use the mark for the goods and services stated in the registration. However, those rights can easily be lost over time if the trademark owner fails to periodically monitor the marketplace. The brand owner must take action against new entrants who are infringers, or whose goods and services are too closely related, or which target the same category of purchasers.

Don't panic. This does not mean you will need to file costly lawsuits to police your marks. However, you may well need to write the occasional letter, or obtain a watch service to notify you or your counsel of recent filings that could be a problem. Contacting infringing applicants early on is key to a speedy resolution before new entrants become committed and have invested heavily in the mark. No discussion of trademark registration is complete without an explanation of the duties imposed upon registered brand owners to police their marks and to maintain registrations.

Trademark Monitoring, a.k.a. "Police Your Marks"

A vigilant brand owner on guard

Trademark registration is merely the starting point. The important tasks of trademark monitoring and enforcement are often overlooked. These are required tasks in order to maintain legal rights in a trademark once they are established. The goal is to ensure that the differentiating thoughts and feelings about your brand are maintained, in order to protect brand equity."

Trademark monitoring includes strategies and a plan to implement them designed to reduce risk and liability resulting from unattended counterfeiting, diversion, tampering, and theft of domains.

What Is Trademark Monitoring; Why Is it Necessary?

Also called "policing your mark," trademark monitoring includes maintaining trademark registrations, as well as monitoring new third-party entrants into the market. Where appropriate, opposing those new entrants that infringe your rights is required. A monitoring program not only protects business value but also bulletproofs the brand from costly legal challenges if attacked.

❦ A mantra for preserving brand value: 'Snooze and you lose.'

A well-designed trademark monitoring program reduces online poaching and maintains brand equity. The objective of policing one's rights is to address third-party uses before a little problem grows into a big one. The cost and effort of an ounce of prevention is less than hundreds of thousands of dollars in lawsuits, or even worse, a complete loss of trademark rights. Read: *5 Easy Steps to Monitoring Your Trademark Rights.*[14]

(1)
MONITOR THE MARKET
FOR NEW ENTRANTS

Companies like CompuMark and Corsearch offer low-cost services that notify brand owners of new trademark and domain filings that may conflict with your trademark rights. Others, such as Mark Monitor, provide more sophisticated web reporting of problems through the use of "spiders" that crawl the web looking for infringing uses of marks. These monitoring services range from monitoring new domain registrations to complete observation of worldwide filings of marks in various countries around the world. These are invaluable tools for legal counsel and brand owners. They serve to alert counsel and clients to new applications before they issue and become problematic. They also provide notice of potential infringing websites before they actually launch.

If you don't know about Generic top-level domains (gTLDs), it's high time you did. There are dozens of new domain endings, making it impossible for brand owners to monitor each domain. However, trademark owners can register trademarks in the Trademark Clearinghouse. If listed

---

14   https://brandaide.com/5-steps-to-trademark-monitoring/

with the Clearinghouse, the Clearinghouse will provide notice to owners of registered marks should there be an attempt to register trademarks in such domains as yourbrand.sucks. Learn more: *Cyber Security for Your Trademark*[15].

(2)
INSTRUCT AFFILIATES
ON PROPER USE

Owners of large global brands have faced the challenges of brand management for many years. Among those challenges is teaching affiliates and the general public how to properly use a particular brand name.

Affiliates include distributors, licensees, and franchisees (and in the Internet space, Internet affiliates). A brand usage and style guide outlining proper use of marks in advertising and marketing in various media is essential in today's world. A style guide provides instruction to team members and stakeholders designed to create and maintain a uniform presentation of brand names across the many media platforms.

Maintaining trademark rights begins in-house, with the owner's use and use by those closest to the brand. It's important that the new brand owner learn the basic rules of the road when it comes to proper trademark use.

---

15   http://brandaide.com/cyber-security-for-your-trademarks/

You are entitled to receive a free copy of the Brandaide Guide to Trademark Use.

> **DOWNLOAD IT HERE:**
> https://brandaide.com/guide-to-tm-use

(3)
ENFORCE A
"NO DOMAIN REGISTRATION" POLICY

Affiliates, distributors, and licensees should *never* be permitted to register domains containing your trademarks. Written distributor, license, and affiliate marketing agreements should spell out this policy clearly. Domains containing your trademarks may be pointed to the distributor's local site. However, ownership of the domain should be closely guarded and held only by the trademark owner. This ensures that if any distributor misuses the domain (for example, to post unrelated products or services at the URL), or if the licensee or distributor is terminated, the trademark owner is in a position to shut down further use.

Policing the Mark is a team effort.

(4)
MONITOR FOR UNEDUCATED, GENERIC USES BY THIRD PARTIES

When you discover others are inadvertently using your mark improperly in editorial content, politely let them know the proper use of your mark. Xerox offers a great model to follow in terms of providing proper use advisories to educate the public. The Xerox ad shown on page 77 is one of many ads Xerox ran over the years to protect its mark from becoming generic as a result of misuse.

5

MAINTAIN
REGISTRATIONS

Trademark registrations require periodic maintenance filings and renewal. Work with experienced brand counsel to calendar deadlines and make certain registrations are not inadvertently lost due to missed deadlines. The two most important deadlines are the following:

- **Declaration of Continued Use.** Between years five and six following the registration date, you must file a Declaration of Continued use, affirming you are still selling the products and services covered by the registration. If you fail to do so, the registration will be canceled. This requirement serves to purge the registry of marks that are no longer in use that might otherwise act to prevent use by others after abandonment.

- **Renewal Every 10 Years.** Before the end of 10 years from the date of registration—and every 10 years thereafter—the owner must file a renewal of the registration. Failing to do so will result in the registration being canceled.

Go to **https://brandaide.com/vaxplan** to insert the dates of your 5/6 maintenance filings and your 10-year renewal dates. Make certain to enter these dates in your calendar, and also schedule a quarterly or semiannual Google search for your trademarks. Consider subscribing to a basic watch service to be forewarned as to new entrants who might infringe your rights.

BULLIES, MONEY SCAMS, AND RIP-OFFS

THE INTERNET ALLOWS ACCESS to the complete knowledge of the world on any given subject with the click of a mouse. Along with access comes the unsavory. Not all the information is accurate or trustworthy, and in the case of trademarks, this includes scam artists, trademark bullies, and in some cases online filing services. Many of these abuses derive from the fact that all trademark filings and the contents of the files are public record. Trademark filings can be accessed by anyone, including phony billing services seeking to dupe unwary applicants.

Be aware of the following:

DISCOUNT FILING SERVICES

In recent years, trademark filing services have cropped up in the form of *legalzoom, Trademarkia, TrademarkPlus,*

TradeMark Express, The Trademark Company, and more. Most offer cut-rate filings with no planning or strategy as to proper filing and no legal opinion as to whether the proposed mark qualifies for registration. Many do not use lawyers to provide the services, and as a result, they are not allowed to give legal advice. To do so would be considered the unauthorized practice of law—giving legal advice without being licensed to do so.

Typically there are no qualified attorneys to develop and draft custom descriptions of goods and services that may result in better protection. Nor will they dissuade you from wasting time and money filing for an unregisterable term.

When it comes time to protecting what is your most valuable business asset, ask yourself:

> *Is the goal to get the cheapest price*
> *but not succeed in protecting my brand?*
> *Or, is it worth a few hundred dollars more*
> *to greatly increase my chances of successfully*
> *obtaining a registered trademark based*
> *upon a plan to succeed?*

Most important, nonlawyers are not allowed to represent you if your application is one of the 65 percent that receive a refusal to register. Applications are rejected for many reasons including the ones discussed previously. Applicants are left to find counsel to respond to the Office Actions.

When filing without an attorney of record, filing services and scammers literally troll the Trademark Office daily to find applicants without counsel. These applicants are solicited for representation by inexperienced counsel. Their clients have no way of knowing whether the quality of the advice is to be trusted or what their chances of success might be.

OFFERS TO RESPOND TO OFFICE ACTIONS

For those who choose to use a filing service to save money, beware! The day after an Office Action issues, you'll receive multiple solicitations from agencies offering cut rates for responding to the Office Action. Offering too good to be true pricing for filing Office Action responses, without having first read or analyzed the nature of the required response is a scam.

One needs to know whether the refusal can easily be overcome. For example, does the response ask for a simple administrative amendment, or does it also contain a substantive refusal that requires legal research and written arguments to properly overcome the refusal. And, what are the chances of success?

THE PHONY BILLING SCAM

❝ Do not respond to unsolicited phony billings for 'watch services' that send invoices for watch and maintenance services with names appearing to be from the U.S. Government. They are scams that only want your money. Proven, reputable companies do not solicit business from brand owners represented by legal counsel whose names are listed on their registrations at the trademark office.

The addresses and emails of trademark owners are public record. A vibrant unregulated industry has developed based upon computer programs that skim the Trademark Office website for the names, addresses, and emails contained in new trademark applications. For this reason, we never provide our client's personal emails in an application to avoid this avenue of scamming. Old fashioned snail mail is another story.

Applicants whose addresses are listed in their applications (and most are) often open their mailbox to find phony invoices for trademark watch or maintenance services. The U.S. Trademark Office does not send invoices to consumers for any reason including renewals of trademark registrations. Watch services can be important but not from such entities as the "U.S. Trademark Protection Agency" or foreign companies seeking payment for global watch services. There are reputable companies that provide these services used by trademark lawyers. Highly regarded companies like CompuMark and Corsearch don't send phony billings to unrepresented applicants. Avoid any company that does so. The latest tact is sending invoices to renew or maintain registrations when no filing is due, an obvious ploy to extort money from the unwary even before there is a looming deadline.

THE TRADEMARK BULLY

The trademark bully is the owner of a trademark that seeks to expand its reach by threats and intimidation of smaller innocent owners of the same or similar name.

Trademark bullies assert claims of infringement hoping those they bully won't fight and will give up what may be valid rights. While trademark owners are required to enforce their rights against infringers, trademark bullies go well beyond the rights they own to assert claims against those selling unrelated goods and services.

Remember our story of Mario. Amazon was a "trademark bully" and likely a "reverse domain name hijacker," terms not yet fully recognized in 2005. Since then, courts have embraced the notion that an innocent domain owner with prior rights can properly keep a domain that was registered prior to the bully's later date of use of a term as a trademark, or one that is being used for goods and services unrelated to those being sold by the bully. We've included a picture of the first page of the lawsuit Amazon served Mario, labeling him a "cybersquatter."

11	
12	IN THE UNITED STATES DISTRICT COURT
13	FOR THE CENTRAL DISTRICT OF CALIFORNIA
	CV05-6960
14	
15	AMAZON.COM, INC., a Delaware corporation,) Civil Action No.
16	Plaintiff,) **COMPLAINT FOR TRADEMARK**
17	v.) **INFRINGEMENT; UNFAIR COMPETITION;**
18	MARIO A. SALINAS d/b/a AMAZON NETWORKS,) **TRADEMARK DILUTION, VIOLATION OF**
19	Defendant.) **ANTICYBERSQUATTING CONSUMER PROTECTION**
20	) **ACT**
21	) **DEMAND FOR JURY TRIAL**

22	
23	1. Amazon.com, Inc. ("Amazon.com") is one of the best-known
24	Internet-based businesses in the world. Its distinctive AMAZON.COM® trademark
25	instantly identifies to millions of consumers its highly successful goods and
26	services. Defendant Mario A. Salinas d/b/a Amazon Networks ("Salinas") has
27	sought improperly to profit from Amazon.com's substantial investment in its
28	trademark and reputation by operating Web sites from the Internet addresses

DOCUMENT PREPARED
ON RECYCLED PAPER

- 1 -

Just because you receive a threatening letter does not automatically mean you will get sued or that the claim is valid. If you ever receive such a threatening letter, obtain legal advice from a *qualified* attorney before concluding you have no rights. The best defense against an online bully is to obtain your own registered trademark before you receive such a notice! Read: *Internet Domain Bully a.k.a. Reverse Domain Name Hijacker* [16]

Now that we have made you aware of the scams and pitfalls of seeking advice from nonexperts or nonlawyers, where can you turn to find professional assistance when you need it? We cover this topic in our final chapter.

16   *Internet Domain Bully a.k.a. Reverse Domain Name Hijacker:* https://brandaide. com/internet-domain-bully-aka-reverse-domain-name-hijacker/

HOW TO FIND
AN EXPERT WHEN
YOU NEED ONE

WHAT QUALIFICATIONS SHOULD YOU EXPECT WHEN YOU HIRE LEGAL COUNSEL?

NO ONE WOULD KNOWINGLY HIRE a foot doctor for a heart transplant. Nor should you hire a criminal or family lawyer to protect your brand. Hiring the right trademark counsel can provide you with a valuable partner in the brand protection process and the overall health of your business. Qualified, experienced counsel should take time to understand your business, as well as review the competitive landscape and third party uses that may conflict with your proposed trademarks. He or she will also provide an honest evaluation of whether your proposed brand name is legally protectable using the principles outlined in Chapter

Two. In short, you are seeking brand counsel that can help craft and review the plan to vax your brand.

Assuming your chosen mark is legally protectable, the next step is to perform a trademark search, followed by an assessment of the search results. This assessment will include an opinion as to the business and legal risks associated with adoption and use of your selected mark and recommendations based upon the results. You should then request a strategy for filings that anticipates potential refusals and assesses the risk of encountering a third party opposition to your application. Brand protection counsel must also have the technical and legal training necessary to navigate the registration process and the potential pitfalls that often arise.

WHERE SHOULD YOU LOOK TO FIND TRADEMARK COUNSEL TO PROVIDE EFFECTIVE GUIDANCE?

There are few opportunities to study trademark registration in U.S. law schools. Most highly trained attorneys received "on the job training" by working for firms specializing in trademarks and from years of experience in trademark prosecution. As a result, finding and hiring a knowledgeable trademark attorney is not always easy, but here's what you need to know in conducting your search.

The International Trademark Association (INTA) is a great starting point in searching for counsel. INTA has thousands of worldwide members, including many attorneys in private practice who are committed to serving their clients with the highest degree of skills. INTA offers one of the **only** sources of professional development for trademark attorneys with an annual meeting providing five days of sophisticated educational legal training each year. An attorney's membership in INTA indicates a high level of commitment to the specialized training and knowledge needed in today's global economy.

Ask if the attorney maintains an active membership in INTA, which is often the most important barometer of the real experience and expertise you are seeking.

State and county bar associations are also a good starting point, but there are only a few states that offer specialization in trademark law. Hence, there is no way to know an attorney's actual experience in the field. For this reason, ask questions. Find out how many filings the attorney has handled, as well as the number of disputed proceedings before the Trademark Trial and Appeal Board that he or she has filed or defended. To further assist you, review *Ten Things to Ask Before Hiring a Trademark Attorney.*[17]

---

17   Part 1: https://brandaide.com/how-to-hire-a-trademark-attorney/; Part 2:
https://brandaide.com/how-to-hire-a-trademark-attorney-part-2/

CONCLUSION

SECURING A REGISTERED TRADEMARK is one of the most important business steps in launching a business, and without a doubt, one of the best investments in the future health of your business. Your brand and its significance to the public is symbolized by the trademarks you select and protect. Your brand may well become your most valuable business asset.

Brand protection is a process, not a destination. A trademark registration is but one step along the path, and certainly not the first step. Before investing in trademark filings, make sure you have selected a term that is strong on the trademark continuum and will qualify for legal protection. Investigate the marketplace, and search for existing third-party users of marks that are identical or similar for the same or related goods or services. This step is crucial to success and will avoid needless legal conflict that can delay or derail the growth of your company.

The trademark registration process can seem deceptively simple. The key to success is to develop a filing strategy based upon the results of your search, or to make certain you hire an experienced trademark attorney who can assist you in doing so. Your plan should be based upon the answers to the following questions.

Exactly what is the mark in which you are claiming rights? Is it words alone, a logo, a composite of the two, a slogan, trade dress, color, or even sound? Are you clear as to why you are choosing one and not another? What goods and services can you protect, and what zone of expansion can be carved out around the mark you have selected? Have you considered how to sidestep potential competitors or conflicting marks that could cause a rejection of your application?

You are much more likely to achieve a successful outcome in the application process with some advance planning and strategizing. And yes, as a result, your application is much more likely to sail through without a hitch!

If you have decided to file on your own, understand how nonlawyer filing services work and the limitations upon the services and skills they bring to the process. Beware of solicitation scams seeking to part you from your cash for no valid reason.

When looking for a real trademark attorney, seek someone who can become a trusted adviser and team member for the long haul. Ask the right questions to find the professional who will help you make wise decisions based upon answers to the above questions.

Finally, please don't make the often-fatal mistake of thinking there's nothing left to do once your mark is registered. Registration is the *beginning* of brand health, not the end. Make certain you instruct affiliates on proper use of your trademarks in marketing materials. Consider a watch search to monitor new filings and potential infringers who will destroy the value of your brand. Calendar important dates for filing maintenance documents and renewals so your registrations remain active and in force. And don't forget to download the free *Brandaide Guide to Trademark Use.*

We hope our guide has been helpful. We wish you great success in your business and in securing brand protection. Remember the three steps:

Select. Secure. Sustain.™

ABOUT
THE
AUTHOR

LEGAL COUNSEL to entrepreneurs, litigator, guardian of big ideas, brand muse, spiritual psychologist. Meet Cheryl Hodgson, founder of Brandaide and Hodgson Legal.

Cheryl provides a unique combination of legal expertise and practical business experience based upon her career in the music industry. Her successful career as a federal court litigator in cases involving music industry contracts, trademarks, and copyrights guarantee strong advocacy in business, calculated to seal the deal while minimizing future risks.

Cheryl oversees brand protection for clients worldwide through her network of trademark professionals. She coaches and trains brand teams on the ideas found in this book. Clients include entertainers, entrepreneurs, publishers, fashion brands, natural food brands, coaches, trainers, authors, music technology, and publishers. When it comes to protection for brands, licensing, and royalties, Cheryl has become the "lawyer's lawyer" to whom other attorneys turn for advice.

Cheryl has served as Professor of Law at Loyola Law School, a Federal Court Mediator, and President of the California Copyright Conference. An avid scuba diver and yogi, Cheryl lives in Los Angeles, California.

CONTACT CHERYL

service@brandaide.com
@brandaide
@cherylhodgson

A PLAN FOR THE LIFE OF YOUR BRAND

This guide will empower you with a plan to safeguard the life of your brand. Bulletproof your assets by following Cheryl's three-step process, and use the Brand Vax Planning Guide that accompanies this book. Make informed selections, avoid the pain of rejection, and secure protection. Build a legacy with a memorable brand, one that impacts the lives of those you serve and helps create raving fans.